true *you*

Other fantastic books in the growing Faithgirlz™ library

BIBLES

The NIV Faithgirlz Bibles
The NKJV Faithgirlz Bible
NIV Faithgirlz Backpack Bibles

FICTION

Natalie Grant's Glimmer Girls Series

London Art Chase
(Book One)
A Dolphin Wish
(Book Two)
Miracle in Music City
(Book Three)
Light Up New York
(Book Four)

Samantha Sanderson Series

At the Movies (Book One)
On the Scene (Book Two)
Off the Record (Book Three)
Without a Trace (Book Four)

Good News Shoes Series

Riley Mae and the
Rock Shocker Trek
(Book One)
Riley Mae and the
Ready Eddy Rapids
(Book Two)
Riley Mae and the
Sole Fire Safari
(Book Three)

The Girls of Harbor View

Girl Power (Book One)
Take Charge (Book Two)
Raising Faith (Book Three)
Secret Admirer (Book Four)

Sophie's World Series (2 books in 1)

Meet Sophie
Sophie Steps Up
Sophie and Friends
Sophie's Friendship Fiasco
Sophie Flakes Out
Sophie's Drama

The Lucy Series

Lucy Doesn't Wear Pink
(Book One)
Lucy Out of Bounds
(Book Two)
Lucy's "Perfect" Summer
(Book Three)
Lucy Finds Her Way
(Book Four)

From Sadie's Sketchbook

Shades of Truth (Book One)
Flickering Hope (Book Two)
Waves of Light (Book Three)
Brilliant Hues (Book Four)

NONFICTION

Devotionals

No Boys Allowed
What's a Girl to Do?
Whatever Is Lovely
Shine on, Girl!
That Is So Me
Finding God in Tough Times
Girl Talk
Girlz Rock

Faithgirlz Bible Studies

The Secret Power of Love
The Secret Power of Joy
The Secret Power of Goodness
The Secret Power of Grace

Lifestyle and Fun

Faithgirlz Journal
Faithgirlz Cookbook
True You
Best Party Book Ever!
101 Ways to Have Fun
*101 Things Every Girl
Should Know*
Best Hair Book Ever
Redo Your Room
God's Beautiful Daughter
*Everybody Tells Me
to Be Myself but I Don't Know
Who I Am*

Check out www.faithgirlz.com

faithgirlz

true you

A *guide* TO BECOMING A FAITHGIRL AND STARTING YOUR OWN CLUB

SUZANNE
HADLEY
GOSSELIN

ZONDER**kidz**

ZONDERKIDZ

True You
Copyright © 2009, 2011, 2016 by Zondervan

This title is also available as a Zondervan ebook.
Visit www.zondervan.com/ebooks

Requests for information should be addressed to:
Zondervan, 3900 Sparks Dr. SE, Grand Rapids, Michigan 49546

This edition ISBN: 978-0-310-754404

Library of Congress Cataloging-in-Publication Data

Hadley, Suzanne.
    Faithgirlz handbook : how to let your faith shine through / by Suzanne
Hadley. — Updated and expanded.
        p. cm. — (Faithgirlz)
    ISBN 978-0-310-72697-5 (softcover)
    1. Girls—Religious life—Textbooks. 2. Christian education Textbooks for
children. I. Title.
BV1546.H23 2012
268'.432—dc23   2011017963

Crafts by Melissa Tenpas
Brain Muffin recipe by Tiffany Wismer
Editor: Kim Childress
Art direction: Cindy Davis
Cover design: Jamie DeBruyn
Interior design: Sherri L. Hoffman
Interior composition: Greg Johnson/Textbook Perfect

Printed in the United States of America

16 17 18 19 20 /DCI/ 18 17 16 15 14 13 12 11 10 9 8 7 6 5 4 3 2 1

contents

Welcome to Faithgirlz	9
Note to the Group Leader	11
Faithgirlz Verse and Promise	14
Week 1 ✳ Getting to Know You	15
Week 2 ✳ Inner Strength	23
Week 3 ✳ Being the True You	33
Week 4 ✳ Revealing True Feelings	43
Week 5 ✳ Inner Beauty	53
Week 6 ✳ Take Pride in Yourself	63
Week 7 ✳ Taking Time for Christ	73
Week 8 ✳ Who Do You Admire?	83
Week 9 ✳ God's Plan, My Purpose	93
Week 10 ✳ No More Mean Girl	103
Week 11 ✳ Standing Up	113
Week 12 ✳ Faith in Action	123

Welcome to Faithgirlz

Growing up isn't easy. With so much to learn and discover, sometimes deciding who you are can be the biggest challenge of all for a young woman. Our entertaining and inspiring Faithgirlz stories have guided tween girls to better understand God's love and promises as they discover "the beauty of believing."

Faithgirlz books, Bibles, and other products show girls that they are children of God and that he has a perfect plan for their lives when they walk with him. By encouraging girls to be who God created them to be, to resist putting others down, to talk to Jesus about everything, and to be loyal to friends, these products strengthen girls to overcome challenges with God's help.

Now you can set out on the great adventure of walking with Jesus by joining a Faithgirlz Club. Starting a club is a great way to get closer to God and others through fun activities, thought-provoking discussions about truth, and exciting service projects.

note to the group leader

This guide contains everything you need to establish and lead a dynamic Faithgirlz Club. Each member should have her own handbook. Discussion questions may be used as group talking points or as journal prompts. Each week will begin with a Bible passage girls should read before the meeting. They may also be asked to bring an item to the club meeting for a group activity.

Getting Started

To get the word out, advertise at your church or send out invitations or emails one month before the club begins. The week before you start, personally call each potential member to remind her about the club and let her know what she needs to bring. Your Faithgirlz Club may be held in a church, in a home, or in any community room with a welcoming atmosphere. To create a friendly environment, decorate the club area with festive objects from a party store. As the club continues, you may want to set aside an area to display girls' art projects.

You'll need:

- at least one Bible
- Faithgirlz™ True You handbook (one for each member)
- craft and cooking supplies
- decorations (optional)
- nametags (if you don't already know one another)
- healthy snacks
- a poster of the Faithgirlz verse (see page 14)
- a poster of the Faithgirlz promise (also on page 14)

A Typical Meeting

Each meeting will begin with a prayer. The leader may pray or ask a girl to pray if she's comfortable. Members will then recite the Faithgirlz verse and the Faithgirlz promise. An icebreaker activity will follow in "Getting Closer." The leader will then give an overview of that week's Bible lesson and follow with a discussion. (Note: discussion questions may be used as journaling prompts.) Girls will then spend some time memorizing the week's verse during "Let's Memorize!" They may also want to recite and/or review the previous week's memory verse. (Incentives may be offered for memorizing all verses.)

Following Bible time, girls will complete a craft or recipe in "Let's Make It!" Girls will then be encouraged in the "Go, Girl!" section to think about how they can serve others in the upcoming week through a specific activity. They will also be invited to reflect on the "Let's Write!" questions, recording their thoughts and feelings in a personal journal.

At the end of the meeting, provide a snack and allow members to socialize for a few minutes. Meetings will run for approximately sixty minutes.

Get Ready for Your First Meeting

If possible, distribute handbooks to the girls prior to your first club meeting. If not, books may be passed out during the meeting. Call all potential members the day your Faithgirlz Club begins to remind them of the meeting time and place. Ask each girl to bring along one object that will tell others something about her. (For example, someone might bring a soccer ball because she plays soccer.) Write the Faithgirlz verse and the Faithgirlz promise on pieces of poster board. You will want to display these in your club area. Prepare craft supplies. You may find it convenient to put supplies needed for each individual project into plastic bags — one for each girl.

Prepare the club area by arranging seating for the girls and putting up decorations. Try to create a welcoming, festive atmosphere for your first meeting. Have some upbeat worship music playing when girls arrive, and give each girl a nametag.

Begin the first meeting with prayer, and then recite the Faithgirlz verse and the Faithgirlz promise. Before moving on to the other activities, you may want to discuss club goals and go over the specifics of meeting times and places, the responsibilities of members, and other club details, such as who will provide snacks, craft materials, and recipe ingredients.

Faithgirlz Verse

So we fix our eyes not on what is seen, but on what is unseen, since what is seen is temporary, but what is unseen is eternal.

— 2 Corinthians 4:18

Faithgirlz Promise

I promise to always ...
Focus on my inner beauty.
Remember that God loves me always.
Love myself the way God made me.
Look at others' gifts without jealousy.
Treat other people the way I want to be treated.
Love my neighbor.
Forgive others when they sin against me.
Love my enemies.
Seek God's will in all that I do.
Focus on the inner beauty of others.

getting to know you

Welcome to the Faithgirlz Club! We're here to get to know one another, learn something new about God, and have fun! Faithgirlz is a club where we will find out together who God is and who he has made us to be. As girls, we all want to be beautiful. The Faithgirlz Club will help you learn how to be beautiful inside and out.

Let's Pray!

Open the Faithgirlz Club in prayer, asking God to guide your time together as you learn more about him and each other.

Let's Recite!

Read aloud the Faithgirlz verse from 2 Corinthians 4:18, and then recite the Faithgirlz promise.

What does the Faithgirlz verse mean? Everything we "see" in this world — pictures in magazines, celebrities on TV, and our friends — sends us a message. But this verse tells us that we are to focus on what is "unseen." There is a hidden world God wants to show us. He wants to give us the secrets to being truly beautiful and happy.

The things we see may promise happiness, but they can never deliver the satisfaction we get from following God's ways. Why is it important to focus on the unseen truths about God? Because those are the things that last forever. A girl may look very beautiful in a magazine today, but in a few years she could look totally different. That kind of beauty doesn't last.

Our Faithgirlz promise talks about the things that will make us beautiful both inside and out. *Beauty is all about God's love!* The Bible says, "We love because he first loved us" (1 John 4:19). God loves us! That's a wonderful foundation to build our whole lives on. Because he loves us, we can love him and then love others. His love helps us take pride in who we are — because we are created in his image — and appreciate the talents and beauty of others. Each week we will recite our Faithgirlz promise to remind us of the kind of young women God wants us to be.

Let's Talk!

What does it mean to you to be a Faithgirl? (Write down answers on a poster board or a large piece of paper.) What goals can we set as a group to move closer to being the women God wants us to be?

Getting Closer

What object did you bring that reflects who you are? Take turns talking about your object and why you chose it to tell others something about yourself. How does the object show that you are different from others? How does it show that you are the same as others?

PERFECT PERSONALIZED LOCKER MIRRORS

Make these marvelous mini mirrors to reflect you!

You'll need:

- scissors
- cardboard or sturdy foam
- scrapbook paper or fabric scraps
- craft glue
- small mirrors (4 by 6 inches)
- magnetic strips
- stickers, magazine cutouts, photos, glitter, ribbon

Directions:

1. Cut cardboard into a 6-by-8-inch rectangle.
2. Cut a piece of paper or fabric large enough to cover cardboard, allowing at least two extra inches to wrap around each edge.
3. Secure fabric on cardboard with craft glue and allow to dry. Take care to have neat corners and a smooth appearance on front and back.
4. Position mirror in center of cardboard backing and secure with glue.
5. Attach 2-by-6-inch magnetic strips on back side of mirror with glue.
6. Decorate exposed fabric with ribbons, stickers, or anything that represents you.

Let's Memorize! ✳ 2 Corinthians 4:18

So we fix our eyes not on what is seen, but on what is unseen, since what is seen is temporary, but what is unseen is eternal.

Let's Write!

Take time to answer the following questions in your journal:

- ◎ What does it mean for you to be a Faithgirl?
- ◎ What things in your life — activities, relationships, belongings — reflect you? What do these things reveal about who you are (your personality, character, or passions)?
- ◎ How can you focus on unseen things — truths about God — as much as the things you see?

Go girl!

This week, talk to one person about what it means to be a Faithgirl.

inner strength

Before Club: Read 1 Samuel 25.

Let's Pray!

Open the Faithgirlz Club in prayer, asking God to guide your time together as you learn more about him and each other.

Faithgirlz Verse

So we fix our eyes not on what is seen, but on what is unseen, since what is seen is temporary, but what is unseen is eternal. — 2 CORINTHIANS 4:18

Faithgirlz Promise

I promise to always . . .
Focus on my inner beauty.
Remember that God loves me always.
Love myself the way God made me.
Look at others' gifts without jealousy.
Treat other people the way I want to be treated.
Love my neighbor.
Forgive others when they sin against me.
Love my enemies.
Seek God's will in all that I do.
Focus on the inner beauty of others.

Let's Recite!

Read aloud the Faithgirlz verse, and then recite the Faithgirlz promise.

Let's Read!

Abby ducked back around the corner. Lila and her friends were standing in the hallway talking about their newest clothing purchases and snickering about the people who dressed like losers. Abby glanced down at her generic tennis shoes. Mom called them practical. They looked nice, but Lila and her friends could sniff out a knockoff a mile away — and they liked to point it out.

Taking a deep breath, Abby rounded the corner and shot a weak smile Lila's direction. Lila looked Abby up and down and raised an eyebrow. As Abby headed for her locker, she heard Lila and her friends explode with laughter. *I wish I could disappear,* Abby thought, her face growing hot. *I'll never fit in, and there's nothing I can do about it.*

Have you ever felt like Abby? Even if you're confident in yourself, the comments and attitudes of others can be hurtful. Some people are bullies. You may not see the factors that cause someone to be a bully, but you can definitely feel the hurtful results. How can you remember who you are in Christ and choose the right path when others treat you poorly or don't do what's right?

There was a woman in the Bible named Abigail who found a godly way to stand up for herself. Abigail

Getting Closer

Give each girl a small handful of M&M's candy. Based on the M&M's in their hands, club members take turns sharing details about themselves. Write down the code on a sheet of paper:

- brown = a fact about your family
- yellow = a nickname
- orange = what you want to be when you grow up
- red = someone who's important in your life
- green = a favorite activity or hobby
- blue = something that makes you proud

was beautiful and smart, but her husband, Nabal, was mean and foolish. At the time, David, who had been anointed Israel's next king, was on the run from Saul, and David's men were using Nabal's land as an outpost. Because they were there, the men protected Nabal's property.

One day David sent word to Nabal, asking that he give David's men whatever they needed. That would be like the president asking your family to host the secret service for dinner. It was a big deal!

Instead of showing respect, Nabal scoffed, "Who is this David? Who is this son of Jesse? ... Why should I take my bread and water, and the meat I have slaughtered for my shearers, and give it to men coming from who knows where?" (1 Samuel 25:10 – 11).

David was angry when he heard about this and planned to attack Nabal and the people who lived in his household.

When Abigail heard what her husband had done, she knew that her family was in danger. So she gathered sheep, grain, raisin cakes, figs, and hundreds of loaves of bread and set out to meet David and his men. When she came to David, Abigail did something surprising: she took the blame.

Falling at David's feet, she said, "Pardon your servant, my lord, and let me speak to you; hear what your servant has to say. Please pay no attention, my lord, to that wicked man Nabal. He is just like his name — his name means Fool, and folly goes with him. And as for me, your servant, I did not see the men my lord sent" (verses 24 – 25).

Abigail took responsibility for the problem. She offered her gifts and asked David not to destroy her husband's household. Impressed by Abigail's wisdom and quick thinking, David replied, "Praise be to the LORD, the God of Israel, who has sent you today to meet me. May you be blessed for your good judgment and for keeping me from bloodshed this day and from avenging myself with my own hands" (verses 32 – 33).

Ten days later, God struck Nabal and he died. After that, David asked Abigail to be his wife.

Abigail understood something important: you cannot control the actions of others; you can only control your own actions. She was wise to do what she could to make the situation better. She didn't blame her husband, even though the crisis was his fault. Instead, she humbly took responsibility and did what she could to make things right.

Abigail had inner strength. She knew what needed to be done and did it. Nabal was a bully. And in the end, God punished him for his unrighteous actions. But God rewarded Abigail for doing what was right: she became the wife of a king!

Let's Talk!

What about you? Do you blame others when things don't go your way? Or do you follow God at any cost and trust him to help you? Think about a difficult situation you're facing with people at church, at school, at home, or in your neighborhood. (Take turns sharing.) How can you stand up for yourself in a way that honors God? What can you do to make the situation better? What difference might it make?

Go girl!

This week reach out to someone who has hurt you or someone you have hurt. Say a kind word, take a minute to smile or give a gift. Don't expect the person to be nice to you in return. Inner strength means doing what's right even when others don't react the way you would like.

Let's Make It!

BRAIN MUFFINS

Packed with nutritious ingredients, this healthy treat will strengthen your mind and body.

You'll Need:

- 1/2 cup vegetable oil
- 1/4 cup olive oil
- 1 small can pumpkin
- 1/2 cup white sugar
- 1/2 cup brown sugar
- 1 cup wheat flour
- 1/2 cup quick oats
- 1/2 cup wheat bran
- 1/4 cup flaxseed meal
- 2 1/2 tsp baking powder
- 1 1/2 tsp baking soda
- 1/2 tsp of salt
- 2 1/2 tsp of cinnamon
- 1 tsp vanilla
- 1/4 cup milk
- 1/2 cup semi-sweet chocolate chips

Directions:

1. Mix together oils, pumpkin, and sugars. Set aside.
2. In a separate bowl, mix together all dry ingredients. Then gradually add dry ingredients to wet ingredients, mixing slowly with spatula.
3. Add vanilla and milk to the mixture and stir. Mix in chocolate chips.
4. Spoon mixture into muffin tins (makes 12 muffins), and bake at 330° F for 35 minutes on middle rack. Do not place near the bottom of oven or muffins will get dry.
5. Eat muffins right out of the oven when they are piping hot, or after they have been refrigerated and are cool.

Let's Memorize! ✳ Proverbs 24:5

The wise prevail through great power, and those who have knowledge muster their strength.

Let's Write!

Take time to answer the following questions in your journal:

- ◉ What does inner strength look like? How did Abigail demonstrate this kind of strength?

- ◉ In what situation or relationship might you need to ask God for inner strength?

- ◉ How can you rely on God to show you the proper path when people criticize you or make wrong decisions?

Being the True You

Before Club: Read Daniel 3.

Let's Pray!

Open the Faithgirlz Club in prayer, asking God to guide your time together as you learn more about him and each other.

Faithgirlz Verse

So we fix our eyes not on what is seen, but on what is unseen, since what is seen is temporary, but what is unseen is eternal. — 2 CORINTHIANS 4:18

Faithgirlz Promise

I promise to always . . .
Focus on my inner beauty.
Remember that God loves me always.
Love myself the way God made me.
Look at others' gifts without jealousy.
Treat other people the way I want to be treated.
Love my neighbor.
Forgive others when they sin against me.
Love my enemies.
Seek God's will in all that I do.
Focus on the inner beauty of others.

Let's Recite!

Read aloud the Faithgirlz verse, and then recite the Faithgirlz promise.

Getting Closer

 Circle your answers to this true or false quiz:

1. My favorite thing is spending time with people. T F
2. I am a good listener. T F
3. I'm good at making people laugh. T F
4. I like to have good manners in every situation. T F
5. In my group of friends, I come up with the ideas. T F
6. I pay attention to details. T F
7. I keep a neat room. T F
8. My friends look to me to make decisions. T F
9. I don't like change. T F
10. When my friends are hurting, I know how
    they feel. T F
11. Sometimes I can be bossy. T F
12. I have a lot of friends. T F

If 1, 3, and 12 are true of you, you have an **otter** personality. You are fun-loving, outgoing, and talkative.

If 2, 9, and 10 are true of you, you are a **golden retriever**. You are loyal, easy-going, and dependable.

If 4, 6, and 7 are true of you, you are a **beaver**. You are organized, self-disciplined, and considerate of others.

If 5, 8, and 11 are true of you, you are a **lion**. You are a determined, confident leader.

Take a minute to discuss your personalities. Are you strongly one personality type or a mixture of two or more?

[Animal personality types developed by Gary Smalley and John Trent.]

Let's Read!

Who are you? Many factors go into making you the person you are: your personality, your abilities, your experiences, your family, and your beliefs. Write down three things you like about yourself:

1. _____

2. _____

3. _____

God designed you as a special person. Psalm 139 says that you are "fearfully and wonderfully made" (v 4). Wow! Think about that for a minute. God made you *exactly* the way he wanted you to be. That means you can love him and serve him in a way that is totally unique! There is only one you.

We live in a world where many people want to be the same. Girls want to look a certain way or wear particular clothes so that others will accept them. Even certain personalities may seem better than others.

Fitting in can be hard, and for many of us, it's a huge dilemma. Some teenage boys in ancient Babylon also faced this dilemma. They had been kidnapped from their own country and were forced to serve a king in a country where people didn't believe in or serve the true God. The first thing these boys were asked to do was eat food that God had instructed them not to. It would have been easy for the teens — Daniel, Hananiah, Mishael, and Azariah — to make excuses for eating the food. Everyone else was eating it, and it didn't seem as if they had a choice.

Instead, the friends decided to take a stand for what they believed. Daniel 1:8 says, "But Daniel resolved not to defile himself with the royal food and wine, and he asked the chief official for permission not to defile himself this way."

God caused the chief official to have a favorable impression of Daniel, but the official was concerned that Daniel and his friends would become sickly and weak from not eating the fancy food. That's when Daniel got creative. He told the official, "Please test your servants for ten days: Give us nothing but vegetables to eat and water to drink. Then compare our appearance with that of the young men who eat the royal food, and treat your servants in accordance with what you see" (vv. 12 – 13).

Has your true character ever been tested? Maybe you were tempted to go along with the crowd or even felt you had no choice. Maybe your friends' answers were just there in plain sight while you were taking a test in school. Being the person God wants you to be may require coming up with a creative plan to stay true to his will for you. For example, you could ask your teacher if you could take the test in a different part of the room.

How do you think Daniel's plan worked out? The Bible says, "At the end of the ten days [Daniel and his friends] looked healthier and better nourished than any of the young men who ate the royal food. So the guard took away their choice food and the wine they were to drink and gave them vegetables instead" (Daniel 1:15-16). God provided a way for Daniel and his friends to obey him and be themselves.

But it gets even better! "At the end of the time set by the king to bring them into his service, the chief official presented them to Nebuchadnezzar. The king talked with them, and he found none equal to Daniel, Hananiah, Mishael and Azariah; so they entered the king's service. In every matter of wisdom and understanding about which the king questioned them, he found them ten times better than all the magicians and enchanters in his whole kingdom" (Daniel 1: 18-20).

Daniel and his friends were at their very best because they remembered who they were and followed God.

Let's Talk!

What about you? When you're faced with a tough situation, do you choose the easy way out, or do you come up with a creative plan to stay true to the person God has created you to be? Remember that God has made you unique, with a specific personality, set of talents, and life experiences that can glorify him. Loving yourself and staying true to God's plan isn't always easy, but it's always worth it!

Go girl!

This week choose three friends or family members to encourage. Tell each friend or family member three things you like about him or her. Focus on character qualities and personality traits, not physical characteristics. (For example: "Megan, I like how you care about people and are a good listener.") You may want to write your encouragement in a card and include a Bible verse that's special to you.

ME TO A TEE

Make a T-shirt that displays what makes you unique!

You'll need:

- dark colored T-shirt (orange, fuchsia, turquoise, navy, or black)
- bleach in a spray bottle
- adhesive scrapbook letters
- foam cutouts
- a large bucket of cool water
- newspaper

Directions:

1. Lay T-shirt on the grass or on concrete.
2. Open up the shirt and put newspaper between the layers of cloth.
3. Using adhesive letters, spell out words that describe you, or write a positive message (example: Go Girl!).
4. Choose cutouts that suit your personality. (You can create your own by cutting them out of foam.) For example, if you play piano, you might use musical notes.
5. Arrange cutouts on T-shirt in a pattern you like; tape them down with double-sided tape, if you wish.
6. Spray front of shirt with bleach as evenly as possible, being sure to cover the cutouts and the empty areas.
7. Allow bleach to soak into shirt for 5 minutes; you will see the shirt color fade. Remove letters and cutouts.
8. Rinse shirt in bucket of cool water to wash out bleach.

Let's Memorize! ✳ Psalm 139:14

I praise you because I am fearfully and
wonderfully made; your works are wonderful,
I know that full well.

Let's Write!

Take time to reflect on the following in your journal:

- Make a list of some of your unique qualities.
  (Examples: I see humor in most situations. I'm good
  at encouraging friends. I'm good at sports.)

- Describe a situation where you would be tempted to
  try to fit in? How can you be yourself in this kind of
  situation?

- Write a prayer asking God to help you be the person
  he wants you to be. Thank him for making you
  wonderful, and ask him to show you how to live for
  him.

Revealing True Feelings

Before Club: Read Exodus 3–4:17.

Let's Pray!

Open the Faithgirlz Club in prayer, asking God to guide your time together as you learn more about him and each other.

Faithgirlz Verse

So we fix our eyes not on what is seen, but on what is unseen, since what is seen is temporary, but what is unseen is eternal. — 2 CORINTHIANS 4:18

Faithgirlz Promise

I promise to always . . .
Focus on my inner beauty.
Remember that God loves me always.
Love myself the way God made me.
Look at others' gifts without jealousy.
Treat other people the way I want to be treated.
Love my neighbor.
Forgive others when they sin against me.
Love my enemies.
Seek God's will in all that I do.
Focus on the inner beauty of others.

Let's Recite!

Read aloud the Faithgirlz verse, and then recite the Faithgirlz promise.

Getting Closer

Split your group into pairs, and interview your partner about a memorable event in her week. (Examples: a test, a special event, a challenging situation, a victory) Each girl will need a pen and paper. Take five minutes to interview your partner using these questions:

- What happened?
- Who was involved?
- How did you feel going through the situation?
- How did you feel about the outcome?
- What one thing did you learn about yourself?
- How might you do things differently next time?

Now take a few minutes to give a "report" to the group about your partner's event. (Note: you can present the information as a news report! For example: "Hello, this is Sarah Jones reporting for 'How Did That Feel?' Today I have the scoop on Hannah Michaels and her amazing birthday party!") Then discuss how feelings affected each situation. Did anyone in the group act one way while feeling something different?

$\mathcal{M}$aggie slumped on the couch. "I don't feel like it," she said, crossing her arms.

"But, honey," her mom said. "You told Mrs. Lancaster that you'd be in the Easter pageant again this year."

"That was before I found out I couldn't act."

"Just because you didn't get the lead in the school play doesn't mean you can't act," her mom said. "People at our church love seeing you onstage."

Maggie bit her lip and held back tears. "I just don't feel like it. I'm not cut out for acting."

I don't feel like it. Have you ever said these words? Feelings, or emotions, affect everything. They affect how you interact with your friends and family members. They affect the decisions you make and the activities you decide to try. They can even affect the foods you eat!

Depending on your personality, your feelings may have a lot of control in your life. They may keep you from doing things you should do. Or they may make you react in ways you shouldn't. Feelings can get in the way of what God wants us to do too. If you don't understand how they affect you, they can become a roadblock to sharing your true self with others or doing the things God wants you to do.

Moses faced this problem. Moses was the guy in the Bible who led the Israelites out of slavery in Egypt. (He also received the Ten Commandments from God.) Day after day Moses went to Pharaoh, the king of Egypt, asking him to let God's people go. Moses went to Pharaoh after the Nile turned to blood, after frogs infested the land, after gnats turned the sky dark, and after God sent seven other terrifying plagues to punish the Egyptians. Moses must have been a brave guy, right? Wrong.

If you rewind to before the bloody Nile, the frogs, and the gnats, Moses was ... a shepherd. That's right. And one day while he was taking care of his sheep, he noticed something strange. He saw a bush that was on fire but didn't burn up. So he moved in for a closer look. That's when he got the shock of his life. God spoke to him! From the bush.

He told Moses, "I have indeed seen the misery of my people in Egypt. I have heard them crying out because of their slave drivers, and I am concerned about their suffering.... And now the cry of the Israelites has reached me, and I have seen the way the Egyptians are oppressing them. So now, go. I am sending you to Pharaoh to bring my people the Israelites out of Egypt" (Exodus 3:7, 9 – 10).

That must have been quite a shock for Moses. After being a peaceful shepherd for most of his life, he would have to storm into town and confront the most powerful man in Egypt. Moses thought God had chosen the wrong man for the job. He told the Lord, "Who am I that I should go to Pharaoh and bring the Israelites out of Egypt?" (v. 11).

Moses didn't feel like doing what God was asking. Maybe he didn't feel adequate for the job. Maybe he didn't feel that people would listen to him or be willing to follow. Maybe he just didn't feel like leaving his life as a shepherd to do something hard. He gave God a bunch of excuses, but the Lord reassured him, "Now go; I will help you speak and will teach you what to say" (4:12).

Moses went on to do incredible things! With God's power, he parted the Red Sea, brought forth fresh water from a rock, and received the Ten Commandments on Mount Sinai. Moses turned out to be an amazing leader. He was the perfect guy for the job, even though he didn't feel like it.

When God looked at Moses, he didn't see a wimpy shepherd. God saw the big picture of Moses' life and everything he would do; Moses just had to be willing to get past his feelings and be the person God created him to be.

Let's Talk!

Have your feelings ever kept you from doing something you knew you should do? Do you have a hard or easy time sharing your true feelings with God and others? Why or why not? Think of a time when you didn't feel like doing something, but you did it anyway. How did God help you?

Go girl!

Elderly people deal with feelings of loneliness and discouragement on a regular basis. With your family or a group of friends, visit seniors at a retirement home or assisted-living facility. You may want to check with your church to see if there are elderly church members you could visit. Bake cookies or take along small gifts or cards. Spend time encouraging some new friends.

GLITTERY, SHIMMERY BATH SALTS

(You may want to do this project over two consecutive weeks.)

How can you look at your true feelings more closely? Get away from the stress, noise, and busyness of life and take some time for yourself!

You'll Need:

- 1 cup Epsom salts
- 1 cup baking soda
- 16 drops food coloring (mix for desired color)
- 1/4 cup of fine glitter
- 35 drops essential oil (try orange, lavender or sandalwood)
- 2 sealable glass jars
- ribbon
- spoon or large-necked funnel
- rubber gloves
- wax paper
- cookie sheet

Directions:

1. Put on rubber gloves.
2. In a large bowl, mix Epsom salts and baking soda.
3. Add essential oil and mix well with your hands.
4. Add food coloring. For purple, start with six drops of blue and eight of red. Mix well.
5. Stir in glitter.
6. When salt has been thoroughly coated, allow it to dry for six hours on wax paper before carefully placing in a jar or bottle; this will reduce clumping.
7. Seal jars immediately and label them according to scents.
8. Keep a jar for yourself and give one to a friend.

To use: Add 4 tablespoons of bath salts to running water for one full tub.

Let's Memorize! ✳ Isaiah 41:10

So do not fear, for I am with you; do not be dismayed, for I am your God. I will strengthen you and help you; I will uphold you with my righteous right hand.

Let's Write!

Take time to reflect on the following in your journal:

- ◉ Make a list of the feelings you experience most often. (Examples: fear, loneliness, uncertainty, anger, happiness, excitement, peace)

- ◉ Which emotions from the list you just made tend to keep you from being yourself and doing what you should do?

- ◉ Look up 2 Corinthians 10:5. This verse talks about how God wants you to handle your thoughts, but it can apply to feelings too. What can you do to let God take control of your feelings?

week 5

inner Beauty

Before Club: Read the book of Esther and bring a few magazines that you don't mind cutting up.

Let's Pray!

Open the Faithgirlz Club in prayer, asking God to guide your time together as you learn more about him and each other.

Faithgirlz Verse

So we fix our eyes not on what is seen, but on what is unseen, since what is seen is temporary, but what is unseen is eternal. — 2 CORINTHIANS 4:18

Faithgirlz Promise

I promise to always …
Focus on my inner beauty.
Remember that God loves me always.
Love myself the way God made me.
Look at others' gifts without jealousy.
Treat other people the way I want to be treated.
Love my neighbor.
Forgive others when they sin against me.
Love my enemies.
Seek God's will in all that I do.
Focus on the inner beauty of others.

Let's Recite!

Read aloud the Faithgirlz verse, and then recite the Faithgirlz promise.

Getting Closer

Using paper, scissors, glue sticks, and magazines, have each girl create a "beauty collage." The collage should primarily feature people but may also include nature pictures, words, and quotes. Have each girl talk about why she chose the pictures she did to represent beauty. What makes these pictures beautiful? Look at examples of inner beauty versus outward beauty. (Example: a mother holding a baby versus an attractive celebrity) What do the images in the world around us tell us about beauty?

Let's Read!

Take this simple quiz. Which sayings about beauty are found in the Bible, and which aren't? Write a *B* next to the sayings you think are in the Bible.

1. "Beauty is in the eye of the beholder."
2. "The king [is] enthralled by your beauty."
3. "Charm is deceptive, and beauty is fleeting."

4. "Beauty is only skin deep."
5. "A thing of beauty is a joy forever."
6. "Bestow on them a crown of beauty instead of ashes."
7. "Age before beauty."
8. "Your beauty should not come from outward adornment."

Our culture is obsessed with beauty. Magazines, television, and billboards splash up images of "beautiful" people. The definition of outward beauty changes through time. In biblical times, very white skin was considered beautiful, and a tan was considered unsightly. During the Middle Ages, women plucked their hairlines to give themselves higher foreheads! Artwork from the seventeenth century glorified plump women with fair skin as the model of beauty.

What are some of the definitions of *outward beauty* today? Remember, the images the world shows as examples of "true beauty" aren't even real. A soap company recently made a video that showed how a picture of a gorgeous woman was created. The woman looked very plain at first. Then stylists did her hair and makeup, and a photographer took her picture. After that, graphic designers used a photo program on the computer to widen her eyes, lighten her hair, whiten her teeth, remove blemishes, and even shave off part of her neck and arms to make them appear more slender! The final picture looked nothing like the original woman.

Answers: Quotes 2, 3, 6, and 8 come from the Bible (see Psalm 45:11, Proverbs 31:30, Isaiah 61:3, and 1 Peter 3:3). The other statements are popular sayings.

As girls, we may be tempted to pour a lot of time and effort into our physical appearance. You may feel that being beautiful on the outside will make you happy. The truth is, outward beauty changes and fades, but beautiful character lasts forever and grows more attractive over time.

Did you know that one of the most beautiful women in the Bible endured twelve months of beauty treatments! When the king of Persia held a beauty contest to choose his new queen, Esther was selected as one of the contestants. For one year, she went through beauty treatments to enhance her outward beauty. At the end of that time, King Xerxes chose her to be his queen.

Though Esther was outwardly beautiful, it was her inner character that was most stunning. While she was queen, a crisis arose for her people, the Jews. One of the king's officials plotted to have all the Jews in the kingdom killed. Because of her position as queen, Esther was able to persuade the king not to harm her people.

Esther's outward beauty allowed her to rise to her important position, but it was her inner strength that enabled her to fulfill God's purpose for her life. Her cousin Mordecai told her, "If you remain silent at this time, relief and deliverance for the Jews will arise from another place, but you and your father's family will perish. And who knows but that you have come to your royal position for such a time as this?" (Esther 4:14).

Esther accepted her calling. She told her cousin, "Go, gather together all the Jews who are in Susa, and fast for me. Do not eat or drink for three days, night or day. I and my attendants will fast as you do. When this is done, I will go to the king, even though it is against the law. And if I perish, I perish" (v. 16).

After this time of fasting, Esther went before the king on behalf of her people, and God saved the Jews through her. For Esther, outward beauty wasn't nearly as important as God's big plan for her.

First Samuel 16:7 says, "The LORD does not look at the things people look at. People look at the outward appearance, but the LORD looks at the heart." We should be most concerned about being beautiful in God's eyes. He doesn't care about the color of your eyes, the kind of clothes you wear, or the shape of your body. He created you exactly the way you are, and you're beautiful to him. Psalm 45:11 says, "Let the king be enthralled by your beauty; honor him, for he is your lord."

Esther's true king was God. And because of that, she was beautiful inside and out.

Let's Talk!

What makes you feel beautiful? Look up Proverbs 31:30 and 1 Peter 3:3 – 4. What do these verses tell you about beauty? How can you be less concerned about your outward appearance and more concerned about being beautiful on the inside? What things are beautiful about you that have nothing to do with physical characteristics?

FLOWER POT

From an ugly seed, smelly dirt, and a plain terra-cotta pot comes something beautiful.

You'll Need:

- 4-inch terra cotta pots
- white glue
- paintbrush
- water
- paper lace doilies
- scrapbook paper cut out to whatever shape or words you want
- scissors
- clear varnish (optional)

Directions:

1. Scrub terra-cotta pot clean. Soak pots in water for 10 to 15 minutes.
2. Cut doilies or scrapbook paper to cover most of the outer surface of pot, leaving some areas blank.
3. Thin out glue with water, using 4 parts glue to 1 part water. Then paint glue onto areas where paper will go.
4. Carefully smooth paper onto pot using wet fingers.
5. Let pot dry overnight or longer until paper and glue are dry.
6. To make your project more durable, varnish outside of pot. (You may want to do this as a group the following week.)

Let's Memorize! ✳ Psalm 45:11

Let the king be enthralled by your beauty;
honor him, for he is your lord.

Let's Write!

Take time to answer the following questions in your journal:

- ◉ Who is the most beautiful person you have ever met? What makes this person beautiful? Does she reflect God's definition of beauty that comes from the heart?

- ◉ What makes you feel beautiful? Do you focus more on inner beauty or on your outward appearance? Do you worry about how others view you? Why?

- ◉ How can you become more beautiful on the inside? Read Galatians 5:22–23. What is a fruit of the Spirit you would like to develop in your life?

Go girl!

Everyone wants to feel beautiful. Offer to give your mom, grandma, or a friend a mini-makeover. Start with a face mask, a foot soak, or a hand scrub. Then offer to paint her fingernails or toes with a pretty polish. You can also create a little gift bag with products to pamper her, such as lotion, nail polish, and lip gloss. Attach a card that includes this week's verse.

Week 6

Take Pride in Yourself

Before Club: Read Genesis 37 and choose two photos of yourself to bring to club.

Let's Pray!

Open the Faithgirlz Club in prayer, asking God to guide your time together as you learn more about him and each other.

Faithgirlz Verse

So we fix our eyes not on what is seen, but on what is unseen, since what is seen is temporary, but what is unseen is eternal. — 2 CORINTHIANS 4:18

Faithgirlz Promise

I promise to always . . .
Focus on my inner beauty.
Remember that God loves me always.
Love myself the way God made me.
Look at others' gifts without jealousy.
Treat other people the way I want to be treated.
Love my neighbor.
Forgive others when they sin against me.
Love my enemies.
Seek God's will in all that I do.
Focus on the inner beauty of others.

Read aloud the Faithgirlz verse, and then recite the Faithgirlz promise.

Let's Read!

What makes you proud? It's okay. You have permission to brag. The Bible warns about pride. But the bad kind of pride comes when you think you're better than others or even better than God. Feeling good about a talent, a physical feature, or a personality trait you possess isn't wrong. In fact, in a way you're praising God for the wonderful way he has made you. So what makes you proud? Doing well in school? Your appearance? Your athletic ability?

When you have healthy pride in yourself, you have confidence. *Confidence* is believing in yourself. It helps you be your best and live as the person God made you to be. Being proud of who God has made you to be is a good thing — especially when you recognize that everything comes from him.

In Romans 12:3, Paul offers this warning about a prideful heart: "Do not think of yourself more highly than you ought, but rather think of yourself with sober judgment, in accordance with the faith God has distributed to each of you." God wants you to have confidence, but he also wants you to realize that your abilities, appearance, and successes come from him.

The story of Joseph in the Bible illustrates this kind of confidence. Joseph had a lot of brothers. Eleven, to

Getting Closer

Take turns talking about your pictures and why you chose them. What about the picture makes you feel good about yourself? What do the photos say about you?

be exact. But for some reason, Joseph was his father's favorite. Parents shouldn't have favorites, but Joseph's father did. And to point it out, he made Joseph a really fancy coat. Joseph wore the coat proudly, and it made his brothers really jealous.

Not only that, but Joseph began having some cool dreams. And he decided to tell his family all about them:

"We were binding sheaves of grain out in the field when suddenly my sheaf rose and stood upright, while your sheaves gathered around mine and bowed down to it." His brothers said to him, "Do you intend to reign over us? Will you actually rule us?" And they hated him all the more because of his dream and what he had said. (Genesis 37:7 – 8)

In Joseph's second dream, the sun, moon, and eleven stars bowed down to him. Joseph proudly wore the fancy coat and told his family about that dream too. This made his brothers really, really jealous.

But Joseph was a good kid. And he told his father when his brothers were up to no good. This made Joseph even more his father's favorite, which made his brothers really, really, *really* jealous. So jealous, in fact, that one day they sold him to a caravan of traders heading for Egypt. Then the brothers soaked Joseph's fancy coat in blood and told their father that a wild beast had eaten him.

Poor Joseph. He hadn't asked to be his father's favorite, to own a fancy coat, to dream cool dreams, or to be punished for doing the right thing, but he was. Thankfully, Joseph didn't give up his confidence. He became a servant of Potiphar, the captain of the Egyptian guard. In Potiphar's house, Joseph became the best servant ever. His master trusted him with everything.

But the day came when Joseph was unfairly thrown in prison. Even so, he did his best there and was soon in charge of the other prisoners. In time, Joseph interpreted a couple of dreams for the pharaoh, which ended up being his ticket out of jail.

Eventually, he became second in command in Egypt. Joseph's confidence and excellent character allowed him to rise to the top. Joseph was confident in his abilities and God's plan for his life. Because of his position, Joseph was ultimately able to save his entire family — including his eleven jealous brothers — from starvation.

Joseph may have started out as a bit of a bragger, but his dedication to doing what was right and believing in himself allowed God to use him in a great way. Ultimately his confidence came from the Lord.

What qualities or abilities in your life do you think it's appropriate to be proud of? Why? How can you balance healthy pride in accomplishments with a humble attitude? Do you think Joseph handled his pride in the right way? Why or why not? What can you do to avoid thinking too highly of yourself?

Go girl!

You have a great opportunity to build the confidence of those younger than you. Proverbs 27:2 says, "Let someone else praise you, and not your own mouth; an outsider, and not your own lips." This week, find a way to praise your younger siblings or other young friends. Recognize one of their abilities or a good characteristic. (Example: "Jackson, you're such a good big brother. I like the way you let your little brother play with your toys.") You can also try this activity with your friends.

MAGNETIC PERSONALITIES

When you have self-confidence, you attract others. These magnets will remind you to stay positive and use the gifts God has given you.

You'll need:

- ◎ a sheet of magnets with one adhesive side
- ◎ a fine-tipped permanent marker or pen
- ◎ white, colored, or patterned paper
- ◎ a thesaurus or dictionary
- ◎ favorite quotes or poetry

Directions:

1. Think of words that describe you — favorite activities, dreams, things you love, family members, friends, your hometown — as well as adjectives that tell about who you really are (loving, friendly, intelligent, etc.).
2. Collect some favorite quotes, scripture, or poetry.
3. On sticky side of magnet, attach paper in fun designs.
4. Using marker, write your favorite quotes, Scripture verses, or words of poetry on paper. Write down words that describe you, leaving space between words.
5. Cut out words and sayings individually so you can rearrange the words to create messages.
6. Place magnets in your locker, on a filing cabinet, or on your refrigerator.
7. Rearrange the words often and remember the great gifts God has given to you. Now go use them!

Let's Memorize! ✳ Psalm 71:5

For you have been my hope, Sovereign LORD,
my confidence since my youth.

Let's Write!

Take time to answer the following questions in your journal:

◎ Write about a time when you were really proud of yourself. What about the situation made you feel good? Were you able to be proud and humble at the same time?

◎ How do you think God might use your positive abilities, characteristics, and successes for his glory?

◎ No matter how talented you are, ultimately your confidence should come from the Lord, and your pride should be in him. Look up Galatians 6:14. What do you think it means to "boast in the cross of our Lord Jesus Christ"?

Taking Time for Christ

Before Club: Read Luke 10:38–42.

Let's Pray!

Open the Faithgirlz Club in prayer, asking God to guide your time together as you learn more about him and each other.

> **Faithgirlz Verse**
> *So we fix our eyes not on what is seen, but on what is unseen, since what is seen is temporary, but what is unseen is eternal.* — 2 CORINTHIANS 4:18

> **Faithgirlz Promise**
> *I promise to always . . .*
> *Focus on my inner beauty.*
> *Remember that God loves me always.*
> *Love myself the way God made me.*
> *Look at others' gifts without jealousy.*
> *Treat other people the way I want to be treated.*
> *Love my neighbor.*
> *Forgive others when they sin against me.*
> *Love my enemies.*
> *Seek God's will in all that I do.*
> *Focus on the inner beauty of others.*

Read aloud the Faithgirlz verse, and then recite the Faithgirlz promise.

Getting Closer

 Give each girl a piece of paper with nine squares. Each square should contain one of the following statements:

- ◎ plays a sport
- ◎ likes to read
- ◎ has a chore list
- ◎ takes lessons of some kind
- ◎ plays an instrument
- ◎ attends church and Sunday school
- ◎ likes to bake
- ◎ has an email address
- ◎ takes care of a pet

For each square, girls must get the initials of another club member for whom the statement is true. A single player may only initial one square twice (so at least five people will need to sign). The first player to get all of her squares initialed wins. Afterward, talk about the activities that fill your day. Do you feel too busy? Not busy enough?

"I'm too busy!" Ashley stuffed her math book into her backpack. "I can't fit in one more thing!" She thought about all the things she had to do that day: school, piano lessons, youth group. She glanced at the Bible sitting on the table next to her bed. "Maybe tomorrow."

Have you ever felt like Ashley? No matter who you are, you probably feel busy. School. Church. Homework. Sports. Friends. All of these things compete for your time. Studies have proven that people sleep on average two hours less than we used to because we're too busy! Maybe you can relate.

As followers of Christ, we're supposed to make one activity the most important in our day: spending time with him. We spend time with Christ as we would with any other friend.

What does it mean to spend time with God? Well, reading the Bible — God's Word to us — is a good start. One psalmist wrote, "Oh, how I love your law! I meditate on it all day long" (Psalm 119:97). *All day long?* That sounds impossible, doesn't it? *I'm way too busy!* But consider this: David was a king. He had some big responsibilities. But he made reading and thinking about God's Word a priority in his day.

The second way to spend time with God is to pray. The apostle Paul wrote, "Pray continually, give thanks in all circumstances; for this is God's will for you in Christ Jesus" (1 Thessalonians 5:17 – 18). How can you pray continually? A man named Sam worked at a newspaper office. Most of the people in the office were not Christians, but they respected and loved Sam.

When someone asked Sam his secret to being a good example at his workplace, he said, "That's easy. I pray continually. I just talk to God about everything that's happening throughout my day."

The third way to spend time with God is to listen to him. John 10:27 says, "My sheep listen to my voice; I know them, and they follow me." Listening to God's voice requires taking time to pause during the day and be still to hear what God wants to say to you.

A woman named Martha learned an important lesson about spending time with Jesus. While Jesus was doing his ministry on earth, he became friends with Martha and her sister and brother. One day, Martha learned that Jesus and his disciples would be stopping by her house. Martha had a plan for how everything would be done. She wanted everything to be perfect!

When Jesus arrived, Martha's sister, Mary, dropped everything she was doing to sit at his feet and listen to him teach. Martha got irritated that her sister wasn't helping. She was so upset that she spoke to Jesus about it: "Lord, don't you care that my sister has left me to do the work by myself? Tell her to help me!" (Luke 10:40).

But Jesus wanted Martha to understand what was most important. He told her, "Martha, Martha ... you are worried and upset about many things, but few things are needed — or indeed only one. Mary has chosen what is better, and it will not be taken away from her" (vv. 41 – 42).

There were many activities Martha could have been busy doing: cooking, cleaning, serving. And these were good activities, but Jesus made it clear that spending time with him was the most important thing she could do. Spending time with him was worth putting aside other activities.

Think about your day. What activities fill it? Do you have enough time to spend with Christ — reading his Word, talking to him in prayer, and listening for his voice? If you don't, maybe God is asking you to give up something less important so that you can spend time getting to know him better.

Let's Talk!

What about you? Are you more like Mary or Martha? How can you make time for God in your day? What less important tasks might you give up to spend more time with Jesus?

Go girl!

Offer to lead your family in a daily devotion for one week. You can read a chapter together—like a chapter from Proverbs (just read the Proverb that has the same number as the day of the month). Then share prayer requests and pray for one another.

SWEETEN UP YOUR JOURNAL

This sweet journal will help you spend time with God each day.

You'll need:

- a plain, smooth-covered journal
- craft glue
- scissors
- decorative items, such as:
    - magazine pictures
    - scrapbook paper
    - scrapbook charms
    - beads
    - stickers
    - die cuts
- adhesive letters

Directions:

1. Cut paper to size and glue to journal, securing edges inside front and back covers.
2. Glue on decorative items to make your journal personal to you. Be creative!
3. Attach adhesive letters to create your name, the word *journal*, or any other word or saying you desire.

Let's Memorize! ✳ Psalm 119:97

Oh, how I love your law! I meditate on it all day long.

Let's Write!

Take time to answer the following questions in your journal:

- ◉ Which is your favorite way to connect with Jesus: reading the Bible, praying, or listening?

- ◉ What is the best time of day for you to spend time with God? Write down a plan to spend time with Jesus once a day for two weeks.

- ◉ What activities in your life are making you too busy to spend time with Jesus? How can you be like Mary and set them aside?

Week 8

Who Do You Admire?

Before Club: Read Hebrews 11; also bring photos of family members and people you admire and some magazines you don't mind cutting up.

Let's Pray!

Open the Faithgirlz Club in prayer, asking God to guide your time together as you learn more about him and each other.

Faithgirlz Verse

So we fix our eyes not on what is seen, but on what is unseen, since what is seen is temporary, but what is unseen is eternal. — 2 CORINTHIANS 4:18

Faithgirlz Promise

I promise to always . . .
Focus on my inner beauty.
Remember that God loves me always.
Love myself the way God made me.
Look at others' gifts without jealousy.
Treat other people the way I want to be treated.
Love my neighbor.
Forgive others when they sin against me.
Love my enemies.
Seek God's will in all that I do.
Focus on the inner beauty of others.

FAMOUS FISH BOWL

Give each girl small pieces of paper, and have her write down the names of three to six celebrities she admires. (You should have about twenty-five characters in all.) Celebrities may be TV personalities, actors, athletes, singers, or Bible characters. Just make sure they're people everyone knows. Fold the papers in half and place them in a bowl. Split the group evenly into two teams.

Round 1: Time each player for one minute, alternating between teams. During round 1, players may say anything but the name of the celebrity to get their teammates to guess. If you don't know the celebrity, you may pass by throwing the paper back in the bowl. Each player tries to get her team to guess as many names as possible during her turn. The round ends when the bowl is empty.

Round 2: Place all the papers back into the bowl. During this round, players must act out the names without using any words. The easy part is that you already know the names in the bowl. The round ends when the bowl is empty.

Round 3: Place all the papers back in the bowl. During this round, players can say only one word. For example, if you're trying to get your teammates to guess Noah, you might say "ark." Be careful! If you accidentally say "um," that's your word. The game ends when the bowl is empty. The team that has guessed the most names wins!

Take a minute to talk about why you admire the people you chose.

Let's Recite!

ℛead aloud the Faithgirlz verse, and then recite the Faithgirlz promise.

Let's Read!

ℋave you ever thought about being famous? If you have, you're not alone. A recent *Psychology Today* survey revealed that 31 percent of teenagers believe they'll be famous when they grow up![1] There are movies and TV shows about ordinary kids who lead famous double lives. Maybe you've daydreamed about being a famous singer or actor.

Or maybe you look up to political figures, athletes, or your own family members as heroes. If someone asked you who your heroes were, what would you say? Write a few of your heroes in the space below. Beside their names, write what you admire about them:

_____

_____

_____

_____

_____

_____

_____

_____

_____

[1] TRU research company press release, January 25, 2001

Who you look up to says a lot about you. You will become like the people you admire. Have you ever wanted to know everything about someone you admired? Maybe you looked up information about this person on the Internet or read a book about him or her. Maybe you saved little articles or mementos — anything that gave you more information about this person.

In Jesus' time, people admired teachers of God's Word. These teachers were called rabbis. A rabbi knew the Scriptures inside and out. Rabbis studied for many years before they were allowed to teach God's Word. Each rabbi had followers called disciples. The disciples not only listened to their rabbi teach; they followed him everywhere! They wanted to make sure they didn't miss anything the rabbi had to say about God.

Jesus was a rabbi and had his own followers. These twelve young men stuck with Jesus for three years while he did miracles and taught people about God. Jesus was the person the disciples most admired, and they wanted to be just like him! By the end of those three years, Jesus' disciples were ready to spread his good news to everyone. They had become like their hero — they knew him, and they tried to think like him and act like him.

When you admire someone, you become like that person. How do you choose your heroes? The writer of Hebrews made a list of heroes in chapter 11. Though the personalities and roles of these heroes were very different, they had something important in common: faith. Abraham had faith to willingly offer his promised son, Isaac, as a sacrifice to God. Moses had faith to lead the Israelites through the Red Sea. Noah had faith to build an ark when not a single drop of rain had fallen.

Think about the Faithgirlz verse for a minute: "So we fix our eyes not on what is seen, but on what is unseen, since what is seen is temporary, but what is unseen is eternal" (2 Corinthians 4:18). All of the heroes listed in Hebrews fixed their eyes on what they could not see: a future with God in heaven. Their actions counted toward eternity because they had faith.

You will become like the people you admire. It's fine to admire a basketball player because you like basketball or to be a fan of a particular singer, but you should also have faith heroes — people you can look up to spiritually.

Of course, Jesus is the ultimate hero. He invites us to be his disciples. He said, "You did not choose me, but I chose you and appointed you so that you might go and bear fruit — fruit that will last — and so that whatever you ask in my name the Father will give you" (John 15:16). Not only is Jesus a person you can admire; he is always with you and will help you be successful. No matter how great your favorite earthly hero is, he or she can never compare to Jesus, our powerful, loving Savior.

Let's Talk!

What makes someone a hero? Who is your favorite hero in Hebrews 11? What made that person someone you can admire? List some of your spiritual heroes. How have they affected your faith and walk with Christ?

PERSONALITY CUBES

You'll need:

- a 3- to 4-inch plastic photo cube
- paper
- photos of family members or friends you admire
- an assortment of magazines, newspapers, or other sources that contain photos of people and groups you admire
- scissors
- glue

Directions:

1. Decide how you want to design your photo cube. Combine photographs, your artwork, and magazine pictures to display six people or groups you admire.
2. Take apart picture cube and use paper template in cube to trace around pictures or paper with pencil.
3. Cut out images and attach to paper squares with glue stick.
4. Put photo cube back together, inserting pictures. Use glitter glue to decorate outside of cube. Write words that describe the people you admire. You can also create designs or outline pictures.
5. Decorate five sides of cube and allow to dry for at least an hour.
6. Finish decorating last side of cube and allow to dry.

Talk about why you admire these people. Who are they? What do they stand for? What do you like about each of them?

Let's Memorize! ✳ Hebrews 12:1–2

Let us throw off everything that hinders and the sin that so easily entangles. And let us run with perseverance the race marked out for us, fixing our eyes on Jesus, the pioneer and perfecter of faith. For the joy set before him he endured the cross, scorning its shame, and sat down at the right hand of the throne of God.

Let's Write!

Take time to answer the following questions in your journal:

- Make a list of your heroes. What do you admire about them? From God's perspective, should you be looking up to them? Why or why not?

- Read Hebrews 12:1. This verse talks about a "cloud of witnesses." These are faithful Christians who have gone before us and encourage us in our walk with Christ by their example. Who is in your cloud of witnesses?

- How can you be a good example to those who look up to you?

Go girl!

Do some research on a famous Christian and tell your family about him or her. To get you started, here are some ideas of people you could research: Amy Carmichael, Billy Graham, Jim Elliot, Gladys Aylward, Hudson Taylor, Joni Eareckson Tada, Fanny Crosby.

Week 9

God's Plan, My Purpose

Before Club: Read Judges 6.

Let's Pray!

Open the Faithgirlz Club in prayer, asking God to guide your time together as you learn more about him and each other.

Faithgirlz Verse

So we fix our eyes not on what is seen, but on what is unseen, since what is seen is temporary, but what is unseen is eternal. — 2 CORINTHIANS 4:18

Faithgirlz Promise

I promise to always . . .
Focus on my inner beauty.
Remember that God loves me always.
Love myself the way God made me.
Look at others' gifts without jealousy.
Treat other people the way I want to be treated.
Love my neighbor.
Forgive others when they sin against me.
Love my enemies.
Seek God's will in all that I do.
Focus on the inner beauty of others.

93

Let's Recite!

Read aloud the Faithgirlz verse, and then recite the Faithgirlz promise.

Getting Closer

Give each girl a piece of paper and a pen and have them create a one-year plan. What would you like to accomplish in the next twelve months? Write down spiritual, emotional, physical, and academic goals. (For example, "I would like to play soccer" or "I would like to read my Bible each morning before school.") Have each girl share her plan and explain why she chose the goals she did and how she plans to carry them out.

Let's Read!

Delany wished she could go home. One hour earlier, she had arrived at Anna's house for a birthday party but so far the six girls had just sat on the couch and watched reruns on TV. There were no decorations, no games, no party favors, not even a birthday cake.

"Ahem." Delany cleared her throat. "I don't mean to be rude, but what's the plan?"

"What do you mean?" Anna asked.

"Well, usually when you come to a birthday party, there's an, uh … *party*."

"Oh," Anna said. "Well, I thought it would be just as fun to just hang out."

How would you feel about attending a party like this? Would you feel like it was a waste of your time? At the least, you would probably feel bored and disappointed. Most enjoyable activities require a plan.

When you play soccer, you must work together with teammates, follow rules and get the ball into the other team's goal. When you make a cake, you must follow the recipe. Even your time at school is planned out so that you can learn specific things during the year and be ready to move up to the next grade.

Without a plan life is frustrating. You might think you would enjoy being on summer break forever, but after a few extra months with nothing to do you would probably get bored and change your mind.

Humans have a natural desire to follow a plan. Did you know that God has a plan for you? Ephesians 2:10 says: "For we are God's handiwork, created in Christ Jesus to do good works, which God prepared in advance for us to do." That's exciting! God has specific plans for you to serve him — specific acts of service that you will do. And the best part is, he will use your personality, talents, and interests to accomplish his will. God is the man with the ultimate plan!

So how do you discover that plan? Sometimes it may feel difficult to know what God wants you to do. The best way to see God's plan for you is to spend time with him so you can recognize when he's leading you.

Gideon was a guy who felt as if he didn't have a lot to offer. His people the Israelites were being attacked by another nation, his family didn't have a great reputation and Gideon considered himself the weakest link. One day an angel appeared to Gideon and said: "The LORD is with you, mighty warrior" (Judges 6:12).

Gideon was pretty surprised to be the one receiving a heavenly message. When the angel told Gideon that God was going to use him to save Israel, Gideon wasn't sure if he was hearing right. He asked God for a sign. "I will place a wool fleece on the threshing floor. If there is dew only on the fleece and all the ground is dry, then I will know that you will save Israel by my hand, as you said" (36-37). The next day, the fleece was so wet that Gideon filled a whole bowl with the water he squeezed out of it. That night he asked for the opposite — that the fleece be dry and the ground be wet. The next day a dry fleece lay on the wet ground.

Gideon went on to lead a small army that God used to defeat Israel's enemy. God had a great plan for Gideon, even when Gideon did not recognize his purpose.

God has a plan for you, too. As you get to know him by reading his Word and talking to him in prayer, you will be ready when he reveals a piece of his plan to you. And as you develop the talents and personality he has given you, you are preparing for whatever the future holds. Whatever is in your future, you can trust that God will do amazing things through you as you follow him. His plans are always best!

Let's Talk!

How do you discover God's plan for you? Can you think of a time when God had a different plan for you than you had for yourself? How did God show you that plan? How did things work out? Purpose is a goal or aim in life. What is your purpose as a Christian? What is your purpose as an individual? If you don't know, how do you think you can find out?

Go girl!

Think of one of your abilities and make a plan for how to use it to serve. Do you enjoy playing with children? Offer to be a mother's helper or volunteer at your church's nursery. Are you a good cook? Prepare a meal for someone who's sick or just needs a break. Are you musical? Play your instrument or sing for a special event.

CARRY-ME TOTE BAG

Personalize this super-cute bag and pack it with your favorite stuff.

You'll Need:

- ◉ two bandanas or pieces of fabric (20-by-20-inches)
- ◉ fabric scissors
- ◉ fabric paint (optional)

Directions:

1 Cut off a 1-inch border from each side of your fabric. Keep this border to make the handle for your tote bag.

2 If you can sew or have someone to help you, you can make a patchwork bag out of various fabrics.

3 Lay out your pieces of fabric with the "wrong sides" together — those sides that you don't want to show on the outside of the tote.

4 Line up the edges as well as you can and use fabric scissors to cut a 3-inch slit every 3/4 inch. Do this on three sides of the tote bag. The top of your bag will not have fringes.

5 Cut a small 1-inch square out of the two bottom corners and throw away fabric.

6 Beginning at one of the corners, take one of the fringes from the top piece of fabric and one from the bottom and tie them together in a double knot. Tie one on each corner. Continue tying all three sides only. Leave a fringe piece at each top corner so you can tie on the handle.

7   Take three of the border pieces you cut off at the beginning and braid them together. Knot the braids at each end and then knot and tie them to each side of the bag.

8   Embellish your bag using fabric paint to write words or create designs that demonstrate who you want to be.

9   Use your tote to carry around your Bible, journal, or anything and reflect on who God made you to be.

Let's Memorize! ✳ Ephesians 2:10

For we are God's handiwork, created in
Christ Jesus to do good works, which God
prepared in advance for us to do.

Let's Write!

Take time to answer the following questions in your
journal:

- ◉ Think of a time when you made a plan. Did your plan
  work out the way you expected? Why or why not?

- ◉ Read Jeremiah 29:11. This verse was written to Israel
  when the nation was in trouble. Do you believe that
  God is good and he cares about you? How do you
  know?

- ◉ Based on your personality and talents, list a few
  things God might have for you to do. (Example, "I
  like to talk. God might have me encourage people
  through my words.")

week 10

no more mean girl

Before Club: Read James 3:1-11.

Let's Pray!

Open the Faithgirlz Club in prayer, asking God to guide your time together as you learn more about him and each other.

Faithgirlz Verse

So we fix our eyes not on what is seen, but on what is unseen, since what is seen is temporary, but what is unseen is eternal. — 2 CORINTHIANS 4:18

Faithgirlz Promise

I promise to always . . .
Focus on my inner beauty.
Remember that God loves me always.
Love myself the way God made me.
Look at others' gifts without jealousy.
Treat other people the way I want to be treated.
Love my neighbor.
Forgive others when they sin against me.
Love my enemies.
Seek God's will in all that I do.
Focus on the inner beauty of others.

103

Let's Recite!

$\mathcal{R}$ead aloud the Faithgirlz verse, and then recite the Faithgirlz promise.

Getting Closer

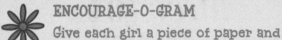

ENCOURAGE-O-GRAM
Give each girl a piece of paper and a pen. Each girl should write her name on her paper. Pass your papers to the right. Write down something you appreciate about the person whose name is on the page. Continue to pass the papers to the right until each girl gets her paper back. Have each girl choose a few comments to read about herself.

Let's Read!

"$\mathcal{N}$o offense, but do you ever wash your hair? It's so greasy." The words were out of Natalie's mouth before she thought to stop them. Brianne and Aubrey snickered. Natalie felt a tinge of guilt for being rude to Jocelyn, but the attention felt good. *She deserved it,* Natalie reasoned. *Her hair is gross! How hard is it to take a shower and use shampoo?*

Natalie watched Jocelyn slink away. "Good one," Brianne said. "She's such a weirdo."

"Just consider it a public service announcement," Aubrey added. The girls burst into laughter.

That's right, Natalie thought, *I was actually helping her.* But already Natalie regretted her words.

Have you ever said something you regretted later? Words are like toothpaste: They come out easily, but it's impossible to put them back in. You've probably known a mean girl. Maybe you've been a mean girl. Mean girls have a hard time controlling their words.

The Bible gives a stern warning about our words. James 3:8-10: "But no man can tame the tongue. It is a restless evil, full of deadly poison. With the tongue we praise our Lord and Father, and with it we curse men, who have been made in God's likeness. Out of the same mouth come praise and cursing. My brothers, this should not be."

Our words can hurt! Words that hurt include gossip, slander, bragging, angry outbursts, rude comments, name-calling, and cursing. These words are like poison. They can ruin someone's reputation, separate best friends, spread lies, or make others feel bad about themselves. As believers in Jesus, our words should be kind, gentle, and encouraging. Proverbs 15:23 says: "A person finds joy in giving an apt reply — and how good is a timely word!" The right words bring joy.

Words that hurt don't just fly out of your mouth for no reason; they begin in your heart. Jesus said: "A good man brings good things out of the good stored up in his heart, and the evil man brings evil things out of the evil stored up in his heart. For what the heart is full of the mouth speaks" (Luke 6:45). A heart that is right with God is the source for words that build up others.

Maybe you've been hurt by a mean girl. And maybe you've wanted to respond by being mean back. Jesus' disciples could relate. They lived in a culture of bullies.

The Romans were cruel to the Jews. They took their money and forced them to serve. Jesus understood this and told his disciples how they should treat mean people: "If someone slaps you on one cheek, turn to them the other also. If someone takes your coat, do not withhold your shirt from them" (Luke 6:29).

When someone is mean to you, don't become like her. Choose to be like Jesus instead. Respond with kindness and love when others mistreat you. Trust that God will be your defender. Think about this verse: "If your enemy is hungry, feed him; if he is thirsty, give him something to drink. In doing this, you will heap burning coals on his head" (Romans 12:20).

It's OK to report a bully. If someone is consistently being mean to you or others, you should tell an adult. But many times, all it takes to make a difference is to give a gentle answer when someone is mean to you.

God did not create you to be a mean girl — he created you to be *his* girl. You reflect him in everything you do. If you're a Christian, it's time to say goodbye to Ms. Mean Girl.

Let's Talk!

*H*ave you ever been hurt by a mean girl? How did you respond? How good are you at controlling your words? Have you ever regretted something you said? How can you make things right after you've said words that hurt?

Go girl!

This week give out your "I-Heart-You Notecards." Don't just give them to friends. Be willing to give a note of encouragement to someone you don't get along with. It may be difficult, but write kind words to someone who has hurt you. After you give out the card, pray for that person for the next five days.

I-HEART-YOU NOTECARDS

Spread love instead of meanness with these nice notes.

You'll Need:

- ◎ fabric
- ◎ white or color cardstock or pre-made cards from a craft store
- ◎ envelopes to fit your card
- ◎ permanent, thin markers or pens
- ◎ favorite quotes or Bible verses
- ◎ craft glue
- ◎ red buttons of various sizes (or pink or white)
- ◎ fabric scissors
- ◎ decorative scissors (optional)
- ◎ scrapbook charms (optional)

Directions:

1. Cut out hearts from fabric and glue them on cards with craft glue.
2. Glue various sizes of red buttons into a heart shape on the front of the card. Or glue on one simple scrapbook charm.
3. Write a quote or Bible verse on the outside of the card.
4. Glue a red button, fabric heart, or scrapbook charm on the bottom left corner of your envelope and write recipient's name on the outside.
5. Write a note inside the card, telling your friend the positives you see in her.
6. Sneak card into your friend's textbook, coat pocket, or lunch bag.

Let's Memorize! ✳ Proverbs 15:23

A person finds joy in giving an apt
reply—and how good is a timely word!

Let's Write!

Take time to answer the following questions in your
journal:

◉ Which of the following types of words do you have
the most trouble with? (Circle.)

> gossip
>
> slander
>
> bragging
>
> angry outbursts
>
> bad words
>
> mean comments
>
> name-calling

How can you correct your words so that they are more
God-honoring? If negative words are consistently
coming out of your mouth, maybe you need a heart
check.

◉ Read Romans 12:20. Write down a plan for how you
should respond to someone who is mean to you.
Think about what Jesus would do.

◉ Have you been a mean girl? Write a prayer to the Lord
confessing the ways you have been mean to others
and asking him to help you live (and speak) for him!

standing up

Before Club: Read Daniel 6.

Let's Pray!

Open the Faithgirlz Club in prayer, asking God to guide your time together as you learn more about him and each other.

Faithgirlz Verse

So we fix our eyes not on what is seen, but on what is unseen, since what is seen is temporary, but what is unseen is eternal. — 2 CORINTHIANS 4:18

Faithgirlz Promise

I promise to always . . .
Focus on my inner beauty.
Remember that God loves me always.
Love myself the way God made me.
Look at others' gifts without jealousy.
Treat other people the way I want to be treated.
Love my neighbor.
Forgive others when they sin against me.
Love my enemies.
Seek God's will in all that I do.
Focus on the inner beauty of others.

Let's Recite!

Read aloud the Faithgirlz verse, and then recite the Faithgirlz promise.

Getting Closer

 WHO IS IT?

Have each girl write down two or three surprising things about herself on separate pieces of paper (example: I rode a donkey). Make sure each girl puts her name on her papers. A moderator looks through papers and asks three girls to sit on the couch. The moderator then reads one of the statements without saying which girl wrote it. The statement belongs to one of the players on the couch.

The rest of the group asks the girls questions to try to determine whose story it is. All three players pretend like it's their story. For example, one girl might say, "My grandpa has a farm, and I rode a donkey when I visited him on summer vacation." Another girl might say, "I played donkey basketball at my school." After questions have been asked, players vote on which girl's story they think it is. Then the true person stands up.

Let's Read!

ᴛake this quick quiz. Which of the following statements are true of you (circle)?

1. I would rather hurt my friends' feelings than do the wrong thing.
2. I have lots of friends, but few know the real me.
3. I quickly defend someone who's being picked on.
4. If I get the feeling others aren't happy with me, I adjust my behavior.
5. I have used a Christian topic for a school project.
6. Most of my friends don't know I'm a Christian.
7. When I see someone doing something wrong, I do something to stop it.
8. I believe you shouldn't offend people by telling them what you believe.
9. I pray and read my Bible in public.
10. If someone is being mistreated, I tell the teacher rather than get involved.

If you circled mostly odd numbers, you have natural courage to live what you believe. If you circled mostly even numbers, you may tend to be shy about your faith.

Matthew 5:14–16 says: "You are the light of the world. A town on a hill cannot be hidden. Neither do people light a lamp and put it under a bowl. Instead they put it on its stand, and it gives light to everyone in the house. In the same way, let your light shine before others, that they may see your good deeds and glorify your Father in heaven."

When you cover up a light, it loses its purpose. God intends Christians to be bright, shining lights that draw people's attention to him. The way we treat people, the decisions we make, and even the words we say should point them to Jesus.

Standing up for Jesus isn't always easy. A girl in Canada named Lia wanted to give a speech at her school about her beliefs as a Christian. Her teacher told her she would not win the competition with her topic. But Lia decided to give the speech anyway. Even though one of the judges walked out, Lia won the competition and advanced to the regional contest.

A man in the Bible made a difficult decision to stand up for his faith. Remember Daniel, Hananiah, Mishael, and Azariah from lesson three. They refused to eat the king's royal food when they were kidnapped and forced to serve in Babylon (Daniel 1). Daniel went on to become a great leader in Babylon. "Now Daniel so distinguished himself among the administrators and the satraps by his exceptional qualities that the king planned to set him over the whole kingdom" (Daniel 6:3).

Daniel's success made the other officials jealous. They tried to find something to accuse him of, but they couldn't because Daniel lived such a good life. Finally they said, "We will never find any basis for charges against this man Daniel unless it has something to do with the law of his God" (Daniel 6:5). They knew that Daniel prayed three times a day in front of his window, so they tricked the king into making a law that anyone who prayed to a god or man other than the king would be thrown into a den full of lions.

This was a death sentence for Daniel. Do you think he considered hiding his faith? It would have been easy to shut his window or find a new place to pray. But Daniel did not make a single change. The Bible says that when he heard about the law, he went home and "got down on his knees and prayed, giving thanks to his God, just as he had done before" (Daniel 6:10).

The other officials easily caught Daniel. And though the king was heartbroken about Daniel's certain death, nothing could be done to change the law. Daniel was placed in the den with lions, and the den was covered with a stone. The king was so distraught, he did not eat or sleep that night.

"At the first light of dawn, the king got up and hurried to the lions' den. When he came near the den, he called to Daniel in an anguished voice, 'Daniel, servant of the living God, has your God, whom you serve continually, been able to rescue you from the lions?'" (Daniel 6:19-20).

The king was overjoyed to hear Daniel's response: "My God sent his angel, and he shut the mouths of the lions. They have not hurt me, because I was found innocent in his sight. Nor have I ever done any wrong before you, your Majesty" (Daniel 6:22).

Daniel's choice to stand up for his faith not only proved his trust in God, it also proclaimed God's power to those who were watching. Following Christ and doing what's right isn't always easy, but Daniel's example convinced a king that God was real.

Let's Talk!

Have you had an experience like Lia or Daniel where you had to stand up for your faith at a cost? What happened? What might have happened if Daniel had refused to pray in a public place? What are some ways you can let your light shine in your neighborhood and school? If you tend to be shy about your faith, what are some ways you can be more courageous?

LITTLE LIGHT
OF MINE CANDLE

This sweet candle will remind you to let your light shine.

You'll Need:

- candle wicks
- pencils
- coffee mugs or glass jars (one for you and one or more to give away)
- gel wax
- glass measuring cup
- pot to melt wax in
- essential oils
- gel color
- scissors
- glitter, small confetti (anything that is not flammable)
- glass beads, marbles or shells (optional)

Hint: Visit your local thrift store to find inexpensive, unique glass jars and mugs.

Directions:

1. Cover work surface with newspaper.
2. Twist the top of your candlewick around the middle of a pencil.
3. Lay the pencil over the center of the top of your mug.
4. Leave wick hanging straight down to touch the bottom of your mug. Add beads, confetti, or other decorative objects to bottom of mug.

5 Follow instructions on package to melt wax. You may want to cut your wax into small cubes for faster melting.

6 Add glitter or small confetti to wax and stir carefully. Add color and scent.

7 Ask an adult to pour the gel wax carefully into the mug or jar. Pour slowly and carefully to make sure the wick stays straight, and pour it down the side of the container to prevent bubbles from forming. Make sure the wick runs straight down the center or your candle will not burn evenly. If it is not straight, just use a pencil or thin stick to straighten it quickly before the wax hardens.

8 Fill the container, leaving at least 1 inch of space at the top. After the candle has cooled completely, use the scissors to trim the wick to about 1/2 inch.

9 Keep one candle and give one away. Remember to always let your light shine brightly.

Let's Memorize! ✳ Matthew 5:16

In the same way, let your light shine before others, that they may see your good deeds and glorify your Father in heaven.

Let's Write!

Take time to answer these questions in your journal:

◎ Write about a time when you hid your faith and should have spoken up. Write about a time when God helped you take a bold stand for your faith.

◎ Luke 6:22-23 talks about being mistreated for your faith. How can it be a positive thing to face persecution?

◎ List five ways you can stand up for Christ in your world. (Example, "I can take my Bible to school and read it during my lunch break.")

1. _____
2. _____
3. _____
4. _____
5. _____

Go girl!

This week speak up for Christ to at least one person. Tell a friend that you are a Christian. Incorporate your beliefs into a school project.

Faith in Action

Before Club: Read Acts 2:42–47.

Let's Pray!

Open the Faithgirlz Club in prayer, asking God to guide your time together as you learn more about him and each other.

Faithgirlz Verse

So we fix our eyes not on what is seen, but on what is unseen, since what is seen is temporary, but what is unseen is eternal. — 2 CORINTHIANS 4:18

Faithgirlz Promise

I promise to always . . .
Focus on my inner beauty.
Remember that God loves me always.
Love myself the way God made me.
Look at others' gifts without jealousy.
Treat other people the way I want to be treated.
Love my neighbor.
Forgive others when they sin against me.
Love my enemies.
Seek God's will in all that I do.
Focus on the inner beauty of others.

Let's Recite!

Read aloud the Faithgirlz verse, and then recite the Faithgirlz promise.

Getting Closer

✳ WHAT ARE YOU DOING?

This is a silly game to get your blood pumping. Write the letters A through Z (leaving out Q and X) on small squares of paper and place them in a bowl. Have two girls stand up and each draw a letter out of the bowl. Read the pair of letters out loud.

Now player one will say, "Natalie, what are you doing?" Natalie must think of an activity that uses both letters. For example, if the letters are B and L, Natalie might say, "I'm building lawnmowers."

Player one must act out the activity (building lawnmowers), while Natalie asks her: "Bekah, what are you doing?"

Bekah may respond, "I'm buttering lollipops." Keep going until one player cannot think of another activity. Then have two more players do the same thing. The crazier the actions and activities the better!

"Lights, camera, action!" When you're making a movie
you have three parts: the lights that illuminate a scene,
the camera that records what's happening, and the
action, where the actors play out the scene for the camera.
Without the action there would be no movie. Sure the
lights and the recording equipment are important, but the
action is what makes an exciting film.

Faith in Christ is similar. You can have the Light—
Jesus—and the right equipment—the Bible, but unless
you're putting your faith into action, God's will for
you won't unfold. James 1:22 talks about this: "Do not
merely listen to the word, and so deceive yourselves.
Do what it says."

There are many ways to put faith into action. Write
a few of your ideas on the lines below:

_____

_____

_____

_____

God's Word is packed full of good things for
Christians to do: love one another, witness, take care
of the poor, stand up for the weak, and do good to
everyone. We have to remember that salvation is not
dependent on the things we do. Salvation is by faith
alone. God loves you the same whether you do 100
good deeds or zero. Ephesians 2:8-9 says: "For it is by
grace you have been saved, through faith—and this
is not from yourselves, it is the gift of God—not by
works, so that no one can boast."

So why do we serve? We serve others to show our love for God. Our good deeds will help others come to know Jesus as their personal Savior.

Christians who lived just after Jesus was on earth were good at putting their faith into action. Acts 2:44-47 paints the picture: "All the believers were together and had everything in common. They sold property and possessions to give to anyone who had need. Every day they continued to meet together in the temple courts. They broke bread in their homes and ate together with glad and sincere hearts, praising God and enjoying the favor of all the people. And the Lord added to their number daily those who were being saved." Because of the sharing, caring lifestyle of the Christians, many people believed in Jesus.

A few years ago, a 12-year-old named Zach Hunter had an idea to serve. His idea came after he read Isaiah 1:17: "Learn to do right; seek justice. Defend the oppressed. Take up the cause of the fatherless; plead the case of the widow."

Zach started a campaign for kids called "Loose Change to Loosen Chains" after finding out that more than 27 million people around the world are slaves. During the first campaign, Zach and his classmates collected more than $8,500 in pocket change for the International Justice Mission.

Although God can use you to do big things, serving doesn't have to be a grand production. Sometimes speaking a kind word, offering to help, or having a conversation about Christ can make a big difference in someone's life.

So what are you doing? These three steps will help you put your faith in action:

1. **Read it!** Go to God's Word to find out the things he wants you to do.
2. **Plan it!** Brainstorm ways to carry out God's commands.
3. **Live it!** Get out and serve others!

You may not start a big campaign like Zach, but you can do great things for God! And when you do, others will want to know more about the amazing God you serve.

Let's Talk!

𝒟o you have an active faith? Why or why not? What can you do to help others know about Jesus? How can you — with God's help — make a difference in the lives of your friends, family members, church, and community.

Go girl!

Plan a service project you can do together as a group. Host a yard work day at the home of an elderly member of your church. Organize a bake sale to raise money for a Christian organization. Collect donations of clothes and toys for a shelter or pregnancy resource center. Find a theme verse for your project, plan the details, and then do it!

BERRY NICE CHOCOLATE COVERED STRAWBERRIES

Share this treat with a neighbor or someone in need of cheering up.

You'll Need:

- dark dipping chocolate (you can use chocolate chips)
- white dipping chocolate
- strawberries
- 1 teaspoon of cream or milk
- food coloring
- waxed paper
- cookie sheet
- microwave safe container

Directions:

1. Clean strawberries, leaving leafy tops. Pat dry.
2. Place waxed paper on cookie sheet.
3. Melt dark chocolate in wide mouth container in microwave. Watch chocolate carefully so it does not burn. Remove the chocolate from the microwave and stir. Heat chocolate until it is smooth.
4. Hold berry by the leafy stem and dip 3/4 the way up berry. Let excess chocolate fall back into the bowl.
5. Lay strawberries on cookie sheet and place in fridge for 20 minutes or freezer for 15 minutes.
6. Create colorful drizzle by melting white chocolate in microwave and adding a teaspoon of milk and 5 or 6 drops of food coloring. Blend with a fork.
7. Dip your fork into the colored chocolate and drizzle it back and forth over the strawberries.
8. Put strawberries back in freezer for 10 minutes or refrigerator for 20 minutes.

Let's Memorize! ✳ James 1:22

Do not merely listen to the word, and so deceive yourselves. Do what it says.

Let's Write!

Take time to answer the following questions in your journal:

- ◉ Complete the following sentence: "I put my faith into action when I . . ."

- ◉ Think about the early Christians. What would it look like for you and your friends to live in a similar way?

- ◉ Look up and read Mark 16:15, Romans 12:13, and 1 Thessalonians 5:14. What good action ideas do you find in these verses?

 faithgirlz™

Bibles

Every girl wants to know she's totally unique and special.
This Bible says that with Faithgirlz sparkle!
Now girls can grow closer to God as they discover the journey
of a lifetime, in their language, for their world.

The NIV Faithgirlz Bible

Hardcover

Softcover

The NKJV Faithgirlz Bible

The NIV Faithgirlz Backpack Bible

Turquoise

Italian Duo-Tone™

Available in stores and online!

 ZONDERkidz™

faithgirlz

101 Ways to Have Fun

Things You Can Do with Friends, Anytime!

In today's world, a girl's free time is precious, but figuring out how to make the most of those spare moments can sometimes be difficult. Faithgirlz! is here to help, with over one hundred unique ideas, activities, and time maximizers you can do by yourself or with your friends. From planning the perfect relaxing afternoon to creating quick and awesome DIY masterpieces, and even tips on hosting amazing sleepovers (complete with lip synch battles and the best-ever snacks), 101 Ways to Have Fun has something for every situation and mood. Whether you have ten minutes or an entire afternoon to fill, finding the ultimate ways to de-stress and kick back with friends has never been easier!

101 Things Every Girl Should Know

Expert Advice on Stuff Big and Small

The editors of Faithgirlz! and Girls' Life have collected their best advice to help girls take charge and feel confident in a variety of situations, from changing a bike tire to talking to your teacher about a bad grade, from being threatened by a bully to falling down the stairs at school. What do you do when you're at a party and you don't know anyone? What's the formal way to set a table (and why does it matter)? This random collection of problem-solving strategies helps with everyday stuff, big and small. With tips, advice, and lots of humor, this is a book every girl needs.

Available in stores and online!

faithgirlz

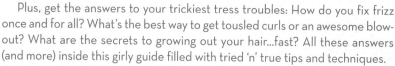

Best Hair Book Ever!

Cute Cuts, Sweet Styles and Tons of Tress Tips

Buh-bye, bad hair days! This complete guide to care, cuts and cute styles makes it easy to have amazing hair each and every day of the week. With tons of tutorials for pretty ponies, bold braids and easy updos, you'll go from school to sports to sleepovers with your loveliest-ever locks.

Plus, get the answers to your trickiest tress troubles: How do you fix frizz once and for all? What's the best way to get tousled curls or an awesome blow-out? What are the secrets to growing out your hair...fast? All these answers (and more) inside this girly guide filled with tried 'n' true tips and techniques.

So no matter what your strand-styling skill level is now, you'll soon be the girl who's showing her friends how to finesse a fishtail or do a double Dutch braid. And what's more beautiful than that?

Redo Your Room

50 Bedroom DIYs You Can Do in a Weekend

Whether you're looking for an all-out room redo or a few new tricks to brighten up your space, Faithgirlz! has tons easy how-tos and quick DIYs that'll morph your room into a true expression of y-o-u. Give your walls a burst of color (even without a bucket of paint!) and turn your fave pics and keepsakes into inspiring art. These floor-to-ceiling secrets help nix those piles of clothes decorating your space in favor of awesome add-ons, like mini murals and a magical ribbon chandelier (psst: we won't tell anyone it took you a half hour to whip up).

Redo Your Room is packed with cute and crafty ways to add pop to your domain. You'll learn how to make even the tiniest spaces into pretty places to sleep 'n' study, and clever ways to keep it all looking adorable. And the best part? You can make over your bedroom without going broke.

Available in stores and online!